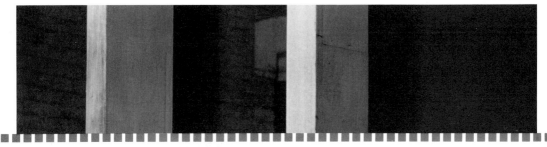

ELVIS IN HOLLYWOOD

ELVIS
IN HOLLYWOOD

Photographs from the making of
LOVE ME TENDER

PHOTOGRAPHS FROM THE
MICHAEL OCHS ARCHIVES
TEXT BY
STEVE POND

A PLUME BOOK

NEW AMERICAN LIBRARY

A DIVISION OF PENGUIN BOOKS USA INC., NEW YORK
PUBLISHED IN CANADA BY
PENGUIN BOOKS CANADA LIMITED, MARKHAM, ONTARIO

Ⓟ

PLUME TRADEMARK REG. U.S. PAT. OFF. AND FOREIGN COUNTRIES
REGISTERED TRADEMARK—MARCA REGISTRADA
HECHO EN DRESDEN, TN, U.S.A.

SIGNET, SIGNET CLASSIC, MENTOR, ONYX, PLUME, MERIDIAN and NAL BOOKS are published
in the United States by New American Library, a division of Penguin Books USA Inc.,
1633 Broadway, New York, New York 10019, in Canada by Penguin Books Canada Limited,
2801 John Street, Markham, Ontario L3R 1B4

LIBRARY OF CONGRESS CATALOGING-IN-PUBLICATION DATA
Elvis in Hollywood : photographs from the making of Love me tender /
photographs from the Michael Ochs Archives : text by Steve Pond.
p.   cm.
ISBN 0-452-26378-6
1. Presley, Elvis, 1935-1977—Pictorial works.   2. Love me tender
(Motion picture)   I. Pond, Steve.   II. Michael Ochs Archives.
ML88.P76E47   1990
791.43'72—dc20   89-77087
                                                             CIP
                                                             MN

Designed by Barbara Huntley
First Printing, March, 1990
1 2 3 4 5 6 7 8 9

PRINTED IN THE UNITED STATES OF AMERICA

ACKNOWLEDGMENTS

Maybe in archaeology three decades isn't a lot of time, but in "rockology" it's almost forever. It's been over thirty-three years since *Love Me Tender* premiered, and not that much longer since the birth of rock & roll. Way back in my first childhood I got to witness the birth of rock music as well as the emergence of Elvis Presley, and I was forced into many a fight trying to defend Elvis. You see, back in the fifties, guys weren't supposed to admit to liking Elvis—that was just for hysterical girls. Real men would never acknowledge liking something so strange. In fact, I'll never forget seeing *Love Me Tender* for the first time. When Elvis gets killed at the end of the movie, every girl in the audience was in tears, while every guy actually applauded.

A lot has changed since then. Now everyone, with the exception perhaps of Albert Goldman, acknowledges Elvis's importance. And the fun of being a professional rockologist/archivist is not so much in finding these rare photos of Elvis, but in putting them in a new context like this book. Now we can all share in the experience of being at Twentieth Century-Fox with Elvis during the making of *Love Me Tender*.

Of course this book would never have come about without the help of the following people: I'd like to thank Allan Licht for finding these rare negatives, Warrick Stone for introducing me to Allan, and Joie Davidow for publishing the pictures in *L.A. Style* Magazine. My friends Stuart Goldman and Adam Taylor were the first to believe that these photos had to become a book and worked tirelessly until it happened. Madeleine Morel did everything a good agent is supposed to do, while at New American Library I had the pleasure of working with Gary Luke as my editor. At Twentieth Century-Fox Films, Chuck Panama and Patrick Miller helped immensely in identifying a lot of the people in the pictures, as did my dear friend Grelun Landon.

I'd also like to thank Steve Pond for the excellent text; and, by the way, Steve Pond would like to thank Bob LaBrasca and Lisa DiMona.

Last, as well as least, I'd like to thank my fearless friends at the Archives, Lynne Richardson, Jonathon Hyams, and Helen Ashford, without whom I could've kept some of the advance.

MICHAEL OCHS
Venice, California

For
John Oakhurst

Love me Tender was Elvis Presley's first movie. It was filmed in the late summer of 1956, during a time when Elvis's records were dominating the pop charts and rock & roll was taking over the music business. It co-starred Richard Egan and Debra Paget, and was directed by Robert Webb, who'd previously made formula westerns like *The Proud Ones* and *White Feather*.

Love Me Tender was a formula western, too, but it also included four Elvis Presley songs. One of them, the title track, spent five weeks at Number One in November and December of 1956. When the movie was released on November 16, fans mobbed the theaters and screamed when Elvis appeared onscreen. Unswayed by the pandemonium, most critics hated Elvis and hated the movie.

Love Me Tender cost less than $1 million to make. It broke even after three days.

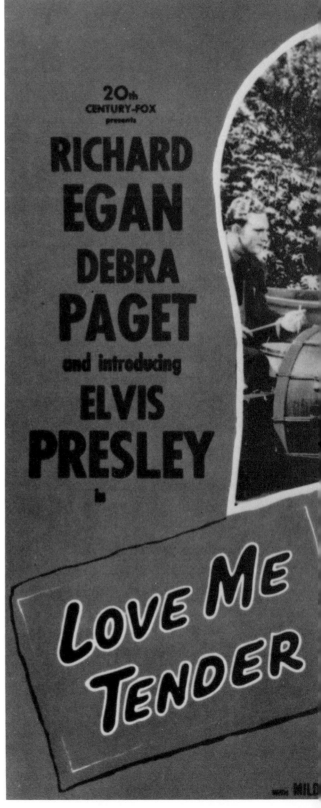

CINEMASCOPE

CO-STARRING

ROBERT MIDDLETON · WILLIAM CAMPBELL · NEVILLE BRAND

NNOCK · BRUCE BENNETT   PRODUCED BY DAVID WEISBART · DIRECTED BY ROBERT D. WEBB · SCREENPLAY BY ROBERT BUCKNER · BASED ON A STORY BY MAURICE GERAGHTY

"I woke up high over Albuquerque/On a jet to the promised land." Chuck Berry wrote it, but Elvis must have thought he was living it.

S OONER OR LATER, THEY ALL CAME to Hollywood. Al Jolson, Bing Crosby, Billie Holiday, Frank Sinatra—one by one, every singing star made the pilgrimage, to test and with luck to reinforce their stardom on celluloid. And in 1956, Elvis Presley came as well.

And Hollywood changed Elvis—or, at least, Elvis changed during the years he spent making movies. He came to Hollywood a greasy golden boy, dripping with sexuality; he left an entertaining, safe icon. Before and after Hollywood, he sang tough, serious songs: "Mystery Train," "Baby, Let's Play House," "I Got a Woman" beforehand; "Long Black Limousine," "Suspicious Minds," "Stranger in My Own Home Town" afterward. But while he was making movies, he settled—not exclusively, but far too often—for the likes of "(There's) No Room to Rhumba in a Sports Car" and "Yoga Is as Yoga Does" and "Song of the Shrimp."

It wasn't all Hollywood's fault. The town dealt with Elvis the way it knew how, as a product to be sold. Elvis's opportunistic advisors encouraged them. And Elvis himself did what he was told; if the thirty-one movies he made could hardly have satisfied him artistically, at least (he could say to himself) they kept him in the spotlight and gave him the money to satisfy his more foolish appetites.

It's not an especially happy story, but

> **He came to Hollywood a greasy golden boy, dripping with sexuality.**

this is only the first chapter. It's a chapter from the days before we knew what the ending would be, the days when, for Elvis, anything seemed possible.

He was The King of Rock & Roll, but that didn't count for much in Hollywood. Not

Awaiting him: a "spontaneous" reception orchestrated by Twentieth Century-Fox publicists . . .

> He was The King of Rock & Roll, but that didn't count for much in Hollywood.

in 1956. Not when the movie industry was still uncertain about what this whole youth craze meant, except that Marlon Brando and James Dean movies made money. Sure, rock & roll seemed to have a place in exploita-

. . . and including six-year-old Linda Williams (foreground), who hounded her father to take her and then waited four and half hours for a tardy Elvis.

tion flicks: the previous year, after all, a low-budget movie about high school hoodlums, *The Blackboard Jungle,* had helped turn the bouncy and innocuous "Rock Around the Clock" into a big hit, and in turn the song drew attention to the movie. But as for the future of this noisy, even vulgar style—well, according to most of the folks who ran the entertainment industry, there wasn't much future, especially not in the polite, repressed whitebread suburbs that Hollywood tried its best to entertain.

Back then, The King of Rock & Roll had a long way to go before he became simply The King. In those days, his title meant less than it would come to mean: Rock was not yet big business, so there were no lu-

"He stopped," she remembers, "chucked me under the chin, told me how cute I was . . .

. . . and I told him how great I thought he was. Then he kissed me. It was the most exciting thing that's happened to me my whole life."

Elvis left LAX the back way. The fans, of course, already knew this. Fox's press agents told them.

crative soundtrack tie-ins and no rock & roll memories to be enthusiastically milked as mood music for sitcoms and dramadies and thirty-second spots. The music was more insular, less universal, easier to dismiss by those not under its spell; for the time being, the new King's domain seemed to have narrow, fixed borders.

But in another way, the crown also meant *more*. In the days before the big business and lucrative tie-ins and enthusiastic milking, rock still bore a sense of danger, men-

Later, Elvis's new stomping grounds: the Fox lot. Behind him, the castle of Robert Wagner—in 1956, aka Prince Valiant.

ace, and libidinous intensity; these untidy impulses bound together those who dared to celebrate them publicly rather than hold them in check. The kingdom had the air of a shared secret on the verge of busting open

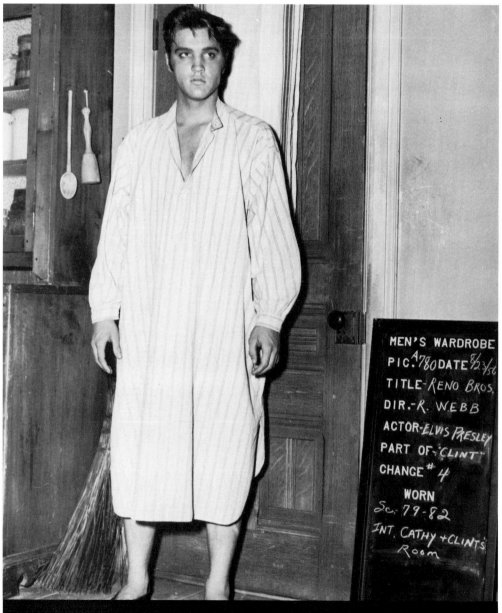

For Elvis, new outfits: no blue suede, no gold lamé, no pink and black.

and the King had vast power and influence, because those who listened closely could feel that he might well be the agent of a revolution. After all, he was certainly stirring things up with the way he moved,

For the movie, soon, a new title: the one on the slate just didn't cut it.

all those palpitations and undulations: They had to be a portent of major change or social disintegration or *something*.

Or you could put it in simpler terms. As one of his subjects said at the time, "He just feels the rhythm. Digs it the most." So they bought the records, and they watched him on TV. He rocked harder than anybody they'd ever heard, and dressed louder than anybody who'd ever come into their living rooms. And in ways they probably couldn't even articulate, they felt free.

He studied Brando and Dean, tried to analyze his appeal:

"I know why girls, at least the young 'uns, go for us . . .

. . . We're sullen, we're broodin',
We're somethin' of a menace."

So the self-styled rebel tried not to grin—and
sometimes, he didn't.

Still, nobody knew what was coming. Elvis had set forces in motion the day in 1954 when he recorded "That's All Right, Mama" in Sun Studios in Memphis, and those forces became unstoppable on January 10, 1956, when he recorded "Heartbreak Hotel" in Nashville. But at the time, he didn't know that himself—and if he suspected it, as he must have, he didn't completely trust his suspicions.

What he knew was that life was getting better and crazier. In less than two years, Elvis had rocked his way from a life of poverty in working-class Mississippi and Tennessee to a brand-new $40,000 house

> In 1956, Elvis knew that life was getting better and crazier.

"I don't understand it, exactly," said Elvis, "but that's what the girls like in men. . . ."

... I don't know anything about Hollywood, but I know that you can't be sexy if you smile. You can't be a rebel if you grin."

(left to right) The Reno Brothers, plus one: Richard Egan as Vance Reno, Debra Paget as Cathy, Elvis as Clint Reno, William Campbell as Brett Reno.

with a swimming pool in a comfortable Memphis suburb; from a dead-end job driving a truck for the Crown Electric Company for $41 a week to a major-label recording contract and thousands of dollars a night for performances; from lonely nights spent listening to other singers on the radio to days tracking the progress of his own single as it picked up airplay. In the first months of 1956, "Heartbreak Hotel" was on the charts, but not at the top: that was the province of instrumentals from Les Baxter and Nelson Riddle; "No, Not Much" from the well-scrubbed Four Lads; The Platters' marvelous "The Great Pretender"; and Kay Starr's "Rock and Roll Waltz," which was rock in name only.

So Elvis and his new manager, "Colonel" Tom Parker, made plans to insure that his new life wasn't snatched away overnight. First, he decided to sing ballads like a hero of his, Dean Martin; he didn't even realize that his own music was helping to make Dino's facile showbiz moves and slick, emotionless music look silly and irrelevant. And Elvis aspired to be a *real* star, like James Dean, whom he'd watched a dozen times in *Rebel Without a Cause*, or like Tony Curtis and Robert Mitchum, the idols he'd admired on-screen during his high school days as an usher at the Loew's State Theater in Memphis. "Singers come and go," said the singer. "But if you're a good actor, you can last a long time."

On April Fool's Day, 1956, Elvis Presley, age twenty-one, came to Hollywood. Intrigued after seeing Elvis singing "Money Honey" and "Heartbreak Hotel" on *The Dorsey Brothers Stage Show*, producer Hal Wallis had suggested a screen test. Wallis was a twenty-five-year screen veteran who'd produced Edward G. Robinson's breakthrough project, *Little Caesar*; Ronald Reagan's favorite from among his movies, *King's Row*;

Several months earlier, in a TV skit: "Really, Mr. Berle, I'll tell you . . .

everyone's best-loved wartime romance, *Casablanca*; and the movies of Elvis's own favorite comedy team, Dean Martin and Jerry Lewis.

Always interested in anything that could make them money, Hollywood was nonetheless not won over by this upstart's raucous music or suggestive onstage antics. Leading the town's assault on Elvis was gossip queen Hedda Hopper, who'd already

. . . the type I dig is someone like that Debra Paget. . . . She's real gone."

branded him "Sir Swivel Hips" and reported after seeing a live show, "I've seen performers dragged off to jail for less."

In this climate, Elvis took the screen test. Playing opposite veteran character actor Frank Faylen—who at one point reportedly had to urge his co-star to stop acting so damn nice and get tough—Elvis ran through scenes from the Richard Nash play *The Rainmaker*. Wallis liked what he saw: "Elvis, in a very . . . modern way, had exactly the same power, virility and sexual drive [as Errol Flynn]," the producer said later.

> "Elvis, in a very . . . modern way, had exactly the same power, virility, and sexual drive [as Errol Flynn]."

On the set, he had what he needed: a director (Robert Webb, in the foreground at right); . . .

. . . other actors (Mildred Dunnock, in shawl) to amuse; a secretary to assist him, courtesy of Fox; and a coterie of pals from Memphis to hang out with.

The games may not have been as much fun as football or fireworks fights (his favorites back home), but they provided between-takes amusement.

The fans were inescapable, but they didn't rip his clothes the way fans did at concerts.

And while the food wasn't quite like his mother's cooking, the Fox commissary was always willing to whip up mashed potatoes and gravy.

Elvis got into singing "because I didn't want to sweat"; moviemaking wasn't hard . . .

. . . but it did involve some manual labor. For instance, when the audience first sees Clint, he's on the Reno family farm, plowing the field with two horses.

Two days after the screen test, Elvis performed "Heartbreak Hotel" and "Blue Suede Shoes" on *The Milton Berle Show*, which was being shot on the U.S.S. *Hancock* aircraft carrier docked in San Diego. One out of every four Americans watched the show. And then Elvis hit the road again, doing another round of concerts and along the way talking to one reporter about his Hollywood experience:

"I spent one whole day plowing mules," he told a Memphis deejay in a phone interview conducted after filming ended one evening. "Man, that was rough!"

Mildred Dunnock, so sweet and motherly, would go on to appear in some fairly gritty films . . .

. . . among them *Peyton Place* and Tennessee Williams's *Sweet Bird of Youth* and *Baby Doll*.

"I took this screen test where I came in and was real happy and jolly and I didn't like it. And then I did this other one where I was mad at this guy and I liked that better—it was me. Mr. Wallis asked me what kind of part I'd like, and I told him one like myself so I wouldn't have to do any excess acting."

While Debra Paget, the picture of fresh-faced innocence, would segue into *From the Earth to the Moon*, *Tales of Terror*, and *The Haunted Palace*.

Six days after the screen test, Wallis signed Elvis to a seven-year, non-exclusive contract to make movies for Paramount Pictures. He was guaranteed $100,000 for his first movie, $150,000 for the second, and $200,000 for the third. They were to be dramatic films, figured Elvis: "Actually," he said, "I wouldn't care too much about singing in the movies."

And then he added, "The dream's come true, you know?"

> "The dream's come true, you know?"

Since leaving Sun Records and signing with RCA, Elvis had had four recording sessions.

This one, which took place in a Fox soundstage/studio, would be his first session outside of Tennessee or New York, and his first without his usual musicians.

It would produce four songs: "Love Me Tender," "We're Gonna Move,"
"Poor Boy," and "Let Me."

Three weeks to the day after his screen test and nineteen days after *The Milton Berle Show*, "Heartbreak Hotel" hit Number One. Elvis's complete domination of rock & roll had begun, and Colonel Parker went looking for a movie project that would be worthy of his boy. Wallis offered Elvis a role in *The Rainmaker*, soon to be filmed with Burt Lancaster and Katharine Hepburn, but the Colonel turned it down. Wallis commissioned a script that would be written specifically for Elvis; this would be *Loving You*, his second movie, but it wouldn't be ready

And as Elvis recorded, Hollywood watched him.

This was before Graceland, before the house with the iron gates. This was a time when Elvis and his folks would let fans gather on his Memphis front lawn . . .

for a while. Finally, Wallis and Paramount lent Elvis to producer David Weisbart and Twentieth Century-Fox to make a Civil War western called *The Reno Brothers*. Elvis was to play the youngest brother in a Confederate family at the end of the war. There would be no singing.

Then again, when *The Reno Brothers* was

. . . so it makes sense that he'd spend time in Los Angeles greeting and posing with any fan who had the connections, or the nerve, to get on the set.

announced, Elvis had just caused an explosion that would rock the foundations of American popular culture. That spring and summer, he appeared on a succession of television programs: *The Dorsey Brothers Stage Show, The Milton Berle Show, The Steve Allen Show.* He swiveled his hips and curled his lip and moved in ways that were bizarrely spasmodic and purely sexual; a few people were horrified, lots were offended and everybody else was transfixed.

Besides, Colonel Parker knew who really paid the bills. At this point, the Elvis Presley fan clubs had about 250,000 members, all of whom received regular messages from Elvis.

A favorite ploy was the giveaway: here, free souvenir packets that would normally cost $1, with the price clearly crossed out so fans know they're getting a deal.

After dinner, Elvis treats his family to some music: (left to right) James Drury as Ray Reno; Paget; Campbell; Elvis; Dunnock; Egan.

He swiveled his hips and curled his lip and moved in ways that were bizarrely spasmodic and purely sexual.

During this time he bombed in Las Vegas, and in one television appearance Milton Berle played Elvis's "brother" as an ignorant backwoods yokel—but even in the face of this kind of scorn, Elvis asserted himself through his music. Four days after signing

his movie deal, he recorded "I Want You, I Need You, I Love You" in Nashville; it

The song's called "We're Gonna Move." The title doesn't refer to his hips.

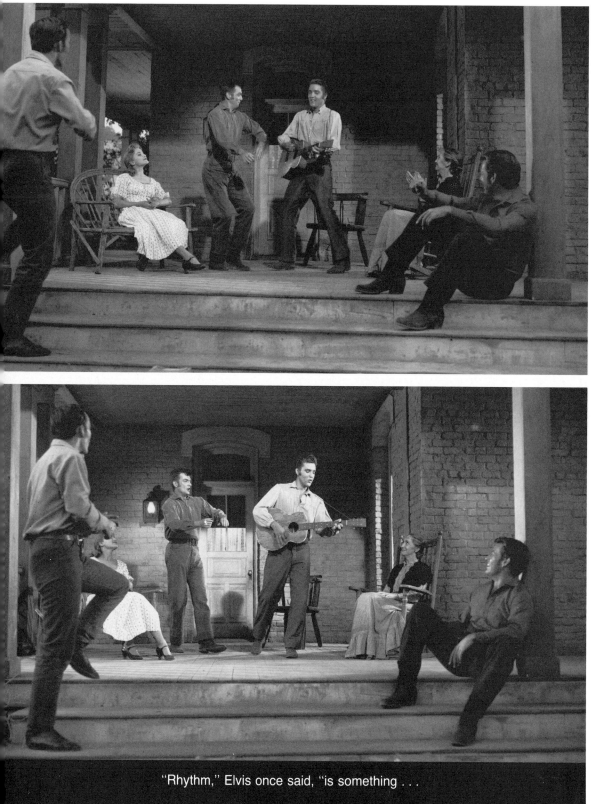

"Rhythm," Elvis once said, "is something . . .

became his second Number One song. In July, he cut "Hound Dog" and "Don't Be Cruel"; they topped the charts for a total of twelve weeks and became the most played jukebox records ever.

From April 26, when "Heartbreak Hotel" hit Number One, until the end of 1956, only three people besides Elvis would hold

. . . you either have or you don't have. And if you have it, you have it all over."

down the top spot on Billboard's charts; Elvis himself would do it with five different songs. In that time, Elvis would be Number One for twenty-five weeks; everybody else (The Platters, Gogi Grant, and Guy Mitchell) would share the position for only eleven weeks.

So when Elvis caught a plane for Los Angeles in August, it was no surprise that

Gyrations over for the moment, Elvis tries something softer.

"I'll be yours through all the years/'Til the end of time."

The Reno Brothers had been renamed Love Me Tender after one of its songs, or that it suddenly featured four Elvis tunes and two completely inappropriate musical interludes.

Elvis flew to town on a late afternoon in early August, 1956. Colonel Parker had told Twentieth Century-Fox that he didn't want any publicity upon their arrival, but a zealous press agent leaked the arrival time to a

> It was no surprise that *The Reno Brothers* had been renamed *Love Me Tender.*

On the Fox lot, Colonel Parker would preside over Elvis's table in the commissary, doling out access.

On the ranch near Malibu, though, things were rougher: folding tables, cardboard milk cartons, and plastic trays for King and commoner alike.

few radio stations and newsreel crews and supplied fans with "PRESLEY FOR PREXY" signs that had been hastily painted in Fox's own sign shop. According to one witness, the Colonel loved it.

In Los Angeles, the first order of business was to record the music. The session took place in a Fox soundstage that had been converted into a recording studio, mostly

Elvis came to the set knowing his lines, Debra's lines, everybody's lines. . . .

for the use of film composers like Lionel Newman. It was a new experience for Elvis: The producers didn't want Tennessee hicks cutting the tunes for their movie, so they insisted that Elvis replace his usual Memphis sidemen, Scotty Moore and Bill Black, with session musicians that included the more genteel and restrained Ken Darby Trio. Ironically, the hired hands sounded more

. . . Back home in Memphis, it seems, he'd prepared by memorizing the entire script.

countrified and down-home on "Poor Boy" and "We're Gonna Move" than Elvis's own musicians had on their recent recordings.

(Darby wrote all four songs in the movie—though "Love Me Tender" is based on an old ballad, "Anna Lee"—but you couldn't tell by the songwriting credits: To make sure

In the movie, they were a love triangle that could only be resolved when one of them died. Posing by a fence on the Fox ranch, they were just three actors working on a movie.

that the proper share of royalties went into Elvis-affiliated publishing companies, the tunes were credited to Elvis and to Darby's wife, Vera Matson.)

If recording the music was at least partially familiar turf for Elvis, making a movie was something else altogether. This was foreign territory, his eleventh-floor suite at the Knickerbocker Hotel, just off Hollywood Boulevard; every night the young rocker would retreat to his room, phone his mother in Memphis, and tell her of his life in Hollywood.

"There's nobody that helps you out," a

> **Every night the young rocker would retreat to his room to phone his mother in Memphis.**

But that changed when the actor on the right took a fancy to the actress in the middle.

Elvis: "I've got one special gal, and she's the only gal for me. But she keeps me 64,000 miles away." Reporter: "Who?" Elvis: "Debbie!"

bewildered Elvis told one interviewer. "They have a director and a producer, [but] as far as the acting and all, you're on your own." And in a phone conversation with Memphis disc jockey Dewey Phillips, the first deejay to play an Elvis record, he complained about the regimen: "The makeup man gets me up at 5:30 every morning," he grumbled, "and I fall into bed at 8:30 every night."

On the set, Elvis did his job, but his Southern politeness and natural deference sometimes got in the way. According to one oft-repeated story, he had particular trouble with the scene in which gun-toting strangers appear outside the Reno house after his brothers have been arrested and taken away. Elvis grabs a pistol and heads for the door of the modest cabin, ignoring his mother—played by Mildred Dunnock—when she snaps, "Put down that gun!" But the first time Dunnock delivered her line, it seems, Elvis sheepishly muttered, "Yes, ma'am," and dropped the gun.

He learned, though. He traveled with a group of his pals from back home, an early version of the Memphis Mafia. And he also made new friends. He hung out with James Dean's old pal Nick Adams, who tried but failed to win a part in *Love Me Tender* on the strength of his friendship with Elvis; romanced his leading lady, Debra Paget, with little success; and rubbed shoulders with Hollywood's brat pack of the time, including the likes of Sal Mineo, Natalie

Wood, Russ Tamblyn, and Dennis Hopper.

And the Hollywood establishment, a group remarkably ill-equipped to deal with Elvis as anything other than a saleable commodity, learned some respect. David Weisbart, who produced *Rebel Without a Cause*, and who talked to an eager Elvis about playing James Dean in a proposed movie biography, compared The Rebel and The King for a

He rubbed shoulders with Hollywood's brat pack of the time.

Elvis pursued; Debra resisted. Elvis asked her out; Debra declined, but said he could come visit.

Debra: "I'll admit . . . before I met [Elvis], I figured he must be some kind of moron. Now, I think the best way to describe his work is to say it's inspired."

New York Herald Tribune writer. No doubt meaning to praise Elvis, he spoke with the mixture of condescension and grudging admiration that much of Hollywood must have felt:

    Both boys were immature, but it was not as easy to spot in Jimmy, who was intro-

And even a sullen, brooding sex symbol . . .   . . . when faced with this on-camera affection . .

. . . had to admit that there's a time to drop the macho facade and enjoy yourself.

A genre convention: you make a Western, you ride a horse.

Later, a Graceland convention, too: Elvis's horses included Rising Sun, Keno, and Star Trek.

verted. Part of Elvis's great charm lies in his immaturity . . . I never got an uneasy feeling about Elvis, because on the surface he seemed to be open and impulsive, but Jimmy was never open, never did anything impulsively.

Elvis was by far the most healthy. Jimmy was apparently the typical confused teenager, but Elvis is something every kid would

> **The Hollywood establishment was ill-equipped to deal with Elvis.**

"Everything stops, and a big, trembly, tender . . .

. . . half smile, half sneer smears slowly across the Cinemascope screen."—*Time*

For the second—and last—time, the conventional plot disappears, and Elvis gets a chance to do what made him famous: shake, rattle, and roll.

like to be—a phenomenal success without having to work hard for it. He's up there enjoying himself and getting millions of dollars. According to a child's logic, what could be better?

Everywhere Elvis went, there were cameras: on the set, in the recording studio,

The band is meant to look old-fashioned, consistent with the movie's time. The lead singer doesn't care if he looks modern; consistency be damned.

"Whenever I see those eyes of blue/ Smiling up so shy," he sang, "I'm in such a spin/ I take right off and fly."

at the airport, in private moments and staged publicity setups. Mostly, it seems, in staged publicity setups. Elvis came to Hollywood to be distributed, utilized, and sold—file him under "TEEN APPEAL," and hope he's got some staying power—and pho-

And then he quivered and pivoted and unleashed that left leg. Onscreen they just clapped and danced; in the theaters, though, they squealed.

"They call me . . . poor boy," sang the recently rich man . . .

. . . "I got a heart full of dreams, and a lotta memories/ And that's enough for me."

tographers positioned the product in appropriate settings. Filming *Love Me Tender* on the Fox lot—most of which is now covered by the skyscrapers and retail stores of West Los Angeles' Century City—or on the studio's ranch near Malibu, Elvis faced Fox's still photographers nearly every day. Some of the photos were used immediately, some surfaced later on album covers and Christmas cards, and some—like many of those reproduced here—sat in studio cabinets and private collections for decades.

Another in a seemingly endless string of photo opportunities: "Okay, let's put Elvis and Debra on the bed, and then she gives him a big box to open . . ."

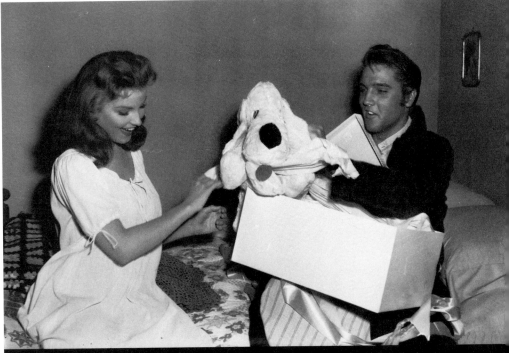

"... No, wait, take that picture off the wall behind them. . . . That's better . . .
Smile, kids . . . Hey, look! It ain't nothin' but a hound dog! Get it, Elvis?"

These photos caught a young Elvis, a fresh Elvis, an Elvis for whom the fatigue and ennui of great fame had yet to become a given. They captured a quality that has most often been described as *innocence*.

And it's at least partially true that Elvis had an innocence about him in those days. Compared to the enervated bloat of his last years, or the mature determination you can see in his 1968 television special, or even the bemused resignation that carried him through, say, *Clambake* or *Harum Scarum*, this is an innocent Elvis—innocent, certainly, to the ways in which Hollywood would waste his talent, co-opt him, and corrupt him and turn him into a screen

> **They captured a quality that has most often been described as innocence.**

Elvis gets it, and then Elvis tries to look surprised and pleased . . .

... though that's an acting job as tough as anything he did onscreen.

He'd already been given so many stuffed teddy bears and hound dogs . . . .

commodity notable mainly for its silliness, and perhaps most of all, Elvis was innocent because he didn't know how little resistance he would raise when Hollywood did it to him.

But look again: This is not a simple backwoods rube adrift and exploited in the big city. At age twenty-one, the fresh-faced Elvis who came to Hollywood had already, in two years, virtually created and then conquered rock & roll. He'd been blasted by critics and denounced from pulpits, and he'd put up with the outrage and the criti-

. . . that in 1957 he could donate an entire truckload of them to charity.

cism like the deferential country boy he was brought up to be.

Still, he knew how to even the score on his own turf. He garnered record-breaking television ratings for any program with the moral laxity to put him on the air—including *The Steve Allen Show*, which dished out a

Vance, Brett, and Ray Reno return unexpectedly from the Civil War after Vance had been declared dead; they're secretly carrying a fortune they've robbed from a Union payroll.

nationally televised, theoretically good-natured humiliation. Allen forbade him from gyrating on camera; dressed him up in a tuxedo and had him sing "Hound Dog" to a basset hound; and stuck him in a comedy sketch with jokes that viciously attacked the working-class Southern milieu from which Elvis came. Elvis didn't say much, though just before showtime he fled the studio and took temporary refuge in a nearby pinball arcade. But the next day, he went into a New York recording studio and took

The tension, of course, mounts: Clint doesn't know that his wife, Cathy, was and is in love with Vance, who's returned home with big plans to marry her.

Late at night: "Cathy, you're cryin'. What are you cryin' about?" "I don't know, Clint. I had a bad dream, I guess. The war and everything . . ."

control, demanding thirty takes of "Hound Dog" until he was sure that the performance was as tough and strong as he could possibly make it. That session, the last time Elvis would ever record in New York, also produced "Don't Be Cruel" and "Anyway You Want Me": three songs, three huge hits.

Elvis may have been insecure in the presence of those who were more cultured or better educated than he, and he may have deferred to his handlers far more than he should have, but deep down, he knew he was a star and knew he was sexy and knew

Blissful in his ignorance, Clint is reassuring: "Don't cry. We're all safe again. There's nothing to worry about anymore." Cathy, nervous: "I hope not."

how to play the game. During the shooting of *Love Me Tender*, Elvis appeared on *The Ed Sullivan Show* for the first time. Sullivan hadn't wanted Elvis on; he was only bowing to commercial pressures, and Elvis knew it. With Charles Laughton guest-hosting for an ailing Sullivan, Elvis sang four songs, including his movie's title track. After the first line of that ballad, Elvis paused for an instant, curled his lip, and

Deep down, he knew he was a star and knew he was sexy.

In another room, Vance lies awake and decides to leave; staying, he knows, wouldn't be fair to Cathy or Clint.

started to hiccup the way he would have during a rock & roll song. A few girls in the audience screamed, just the way he knew they would. He grinned—it was just a quick, small grin, easy to miss—and then slid back into the song without missing a beat. This was not the work of an innocent, but of a master showman who knew how to work a crowd.

Elvis could work a crowd of one, as well.

The Reno family goes to a carnival, where Clint's remarkable, hip-swivelling brand of sixties rock & roll—you know: 1860s rock & roll—is a featured attraction.

Vance, meanwhile, makes plans to leave for California. He tells Cathy; she takes it hard. He tells Clint; his trusting baby brother still doesn't understand what's happening.

Known for revealing nothing and being unfailingly polite in interviews, he was sometimes playfully arrogant. There's a 1956 account, for instance, of Elvis in Hollywood from a young female writer for a New York newspaper:

A press agent came by to tell me I had had enough time with Elvis. I started to leave and Elvis, who was still sprawled on the couch, darted out his hand and caught my foot. "Maybe she's shy; maybe she'd like to be alone with me," he said. The press agent shrugged and left.

I asked Elvis to take his hand off my foot. "Okay," he said, looking up under heavy lids. "Ah'm just spoofing you." I asked Elvis how he felt about girls who threw themselves at him. Again the heavy-lidded look. "Ah usually take them," he said, watching my face for the shock value of his words. He grinned. "Hell," he said, "you know, Ah'm kind of having fun with you because you're so smart."

This was not Elvis the Innocent; this was Elvis in command. At this point Elvis's career had the potential to end quickly, or the potential to remain vital for decades; at the time, nothing suggested that it would tail off into a string of foolish movies, half-hearted records, and, over and over again, stunning rallies. Earnest and muddled, *Love Me Tender* was anything but conclusive: It wasn't very good, of course, but there was a

The plot, as they say, thickens: federal agents arrive and demand their stolen money back. Vance, Ray, and Brett are arrested.

certain charm to Elvis' screen presence and a talent that showed signs of developing.

The problem, though, was that there was never any *need* to develop that talent. *Love Me Tender* opened in November of 1956 in 550 theaters—nothing compared to the way blockbusters saturate the market with 2,000 prints these days, but at the time an almost unprecedented number of screens. Most

Clint's still confused: he doesn't know why his brothers were arrested, why Vance was making plans to leave, and why his wife's acting strange.

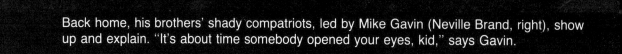

Back home, his brothers' shady compatriots, led by Mike Gavin (Neville Brand, right), show up and explain. "It's about time somebody opened your eyes, kid," says Gavin.

critics hated it: *Time* still gets the award for the most often-quoted Elvis putdown with a review that began, "Is it a sausage? It is certainly smooth and damp looking, but who ever heard of a 172-lb. sausage 6 ft. tall?" And despite what the critics said, before a single week was out *Love Me Tender* had earned back its $1 million cost.

The quality of Elvis's movies quickly became almost incidental. His next few films were among his best: *Loving You* had great music to support its tale of a country boy who becomes a rock star; *Jailhouse Rock* let Elvis act mean and sing more terrific songs; *King Creole* was short on top-drawer music, but Elvis showed signs of becoming a creditable actor; *G.I. Blues* wasn't much, but you could give the guy a break because he'd just gotten out of the army.

Then Elvis began his unstoppable slide into schlock. Elvis didn't like *G.I. Blues* and put pressure on Colonel Parker to get him a *real* movie role; the Colonel responded with *Flaming Star*, his first Western since *Love Me Tender*, and one of the few films in which drama took precedence over music. *Wild in the Country* followed; again, music was deemphasized in favor of a downbeat script by playwright Clifford Odets. Neither of those films won rave reviews; and neither made as much money as the Colonel or the studio would have liked. And then came *Blue Hawaii*, the movie that effectively ended Elvis's chance to have a serious film career: scenic, shallow and stupid, even if it did contain a signature song in "Can't Help Falling in Love," this was the movie that conclusively proved to Elvis and the Colonel that dumb, quickie travelogues were all they needed to pay the bills.

And Elvis went along with it. His eyes glazed over, he stopped even trying to act, and he slowly became someone whose look and manner would have been scarcely recognizable had we not watched every step of the transition. He made movies that were

Clint learns of the stolen money. Then he learns of Vance and Cathy's love.

embarrassing and unwatchable, but for the perverse sense of fun—mixed, of course, with sheer horror—that came from seeing *Elvis Presley* breezing his way through the good-natured inanity of, say, *Kissin' Cousins*. In between his few quality recordings, he

And now he's mad. Really mad. "Tell me he's never had you in his arms since he came back!" he screams. "You can't say it, because it's true! *You lied to me!*"

He made movies that
were embarrassing and
unwatchable.

We're in the homestretch, and things are getting complicated. Vance is trying to return the money and get the charges dropped, but Gavin thinks he's absconding with the loot.

Cathy heads for the hills to meet Vance. Clint and Gavin go to stop Vance. Ray and Brett go to stop Clint. Vance goes there to fix everything . . .

cut kitsch classics that would have once been unthinkable from the man responsible for "That's All Right, Mama," and unlikely from the man who made "Hound Dog."

At some point during his time in Hollywood, Elvis Presley achieved what he wanted:

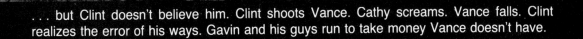

... but Clint doesn't believe him. Clint shoots Vance. Cathy screams. Vance falls. Clint realizes the error of his ways. Gavin and his guys run to take money Vance doesn't have.

Clint shoots at Gavin to make him stop. Gavin shoots back. Clint falls. Gavin runs away and is immediately caught by the Feds. Vance recovers, and he and Cathy run to Clint.

He stopped being The King of Rock & Roll, and became simply The King. There were always moments of revelation, especially for a time after 1968, when he rocked as hard as he ever had, but for the most part, you could say that if Elvis still had the power to rock & roll, he had lost some of the will to do so.

Now the man is a dozen years gone, and the commodity is doing better than ever. In

"Now, everything's gonna be all right." Clint breathes his last. In the theaters, meanwhile, teenage girls cried. Their boyfriends, not quite so broken up, clapped.

death, Elvis makes more money each year than he ever made during his lifetime, and generates at least as much interest as he had at any time since his mid-Fifties stint as a threat to civilization. Witness the incessant tabloid stories: "Elvis Is Alive," "Elvis's Secret Hideout Revealed," "Caveman Looked Like Elvis." Witness the re-

Director Robert Webb, in baseball cap, confers with Elvis and Richard Egan.

Robert Webb would continue directing—*The Way to the Gold*, *The Capetown Affair*, the colorfully named *Seven Women from Hell*—but nothing else would turn a profit as fast.

Elvis gets paid $1,000 a day, or thereabouts. "Of course," says a Fox staffer, "Elvis wouldn't really have had to go to the cash window to get his paycheck."

cords, a constant stream of reissues and repackagings, some remarkable and some redundant. Witness the books.

Or witness the house. Elvis didn't even own Graceland when he came to Hollywood to make *Love Me Tender*; back then he and his parents lived in a comfortable, one-story ranch house on a tree-lined suburban street on the outskirts of Memphis. In early 1957, though, he'd make the move to the two-story mansion that now sits on Elvis Presley Boulevard; the house whose grounds

Elvis earns his paycheck with the old grip 'n' grin: being nice, trading small talk, and posing with the right people . . . like Marie (Mrs. Tom) Parker.

are fronted by a stone wall covered with Elvis-related graffiti; the house from whose windows you can look across the street to the shopping center made up entirely of the Graceland tour center, the Heartbreak Hotel restaurant, and about a dozen Elvis souvenir shops; the house that attracts 650,000 people a year and brings in two-thirds of the $15 million generated by the Presley estate each year.

The figures make it sound lively—but in truth, much of the time Graceland is a gray,

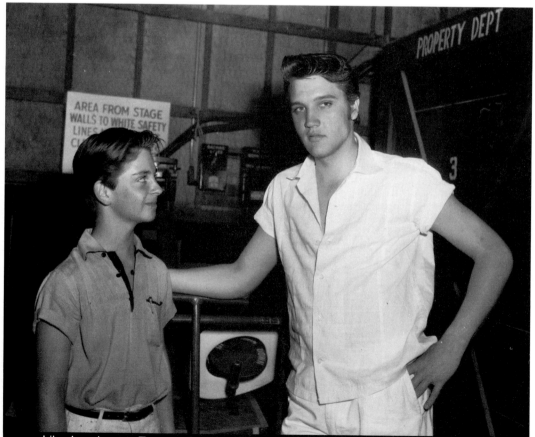

. . . Like Lassie star Tommy Rettig, who spent a day on the set. "He said he'd seen Lassie a few times," says Rettig, "and I told him I loved his music."

. . . Like Neil Ray, legman/reporter for gossip queen Louella Parsons. Archrival Hedda Hopper was a staunch Elvis critic, so Parsons was kinder.

depressing place. The trees are often barren and the grass yellow, but that's just winter in Memphis. But worse than that, Elvis's old home has lost even the appalling, tacky vitality that once made it a curiously fitting shrine to a man with lousy taste, voracious

. . . Like executives from RCA Records and the record industry at large. Colonel Parker, as was his inexplicable habit from time to time, donned a phony goatee for the occasion.

appetites, and, oh yeah, enormous talent. Now, the Elvis souvenirs have become boring: cheap, but without the consummate cheesiness that you used to find in Elvis-head slippers and *Blue Hawaii* music box whiskey decanters. In a way, the place is the final triumph of the process that Colonel Parker raised to an art form, with lots of help from Hollywood and precious little resistance from Elvis himself: The King as a commodity.

But look at the bits and pieces he left

. . . Like Bill Bullock (left) and Steve Sholes (right). Bullock was an executive at RCA; Sholes signed Elvis to the label and frequently produced him.

behind from those days in Hollywood, and
you can begin to find the talent that made
that exploitation possible to begin with.

. . . And like the advisors, businessmen, and
associates who surrounded him everywhere.

Watch *Love Me Tender*, fast-forwarding
through the endless shots of people riding
one direction, then another; lousy as the

They basked in the starglow of their boy;
Elvis tried not to look too uncomfortable.

movie is, it's also likeable. Listen to the songs Elvis recorded in Hollywood during the making of the movie—not so much the four that are used in the film, but the thirteen he recorded in three days in early September: "Paralyzed," "Long Tall Sally," "Too Much," "Rip It Up," "Love Me," "When My Blue Moon Turns to Gold Again," "Ready Teddy," "Playing for Keeps," "How's the World Treating You," "First in Line," and several others. And look at these photos: Even when they're posed and stilted, there's an awesomely gifted twenty-one-year-old rock & roller on display.

Feel the rhythm. Dig him the most.

> Talent made that exploitation possible to begin with.

In the end, The King of Rock & Roll finds a refuge: close your eyes and play your music.

Love Me Tender
November, 1956—Twentieth Century-Fox
Produced by David Weisbart, directed by Robert D. Webb, starring Richard Egan, Debra Paget, Elvis Presley.

Loving You
July, 1957—Paramount
Produced by Hal Wallis, directed by Hal Kanter, starring Elvis Presley, Lizabeth Scott, Wendell Corey, Dolores Hart.

Jailhouse Rock
October, 1957—Twentieth Century-Fox
Produced by Pandro S. Berman, directed by Richard Thorpe, starring Elvis Presley, Judy Tyler, Mickey Shaughnessy, Dean Jones.

King Creole
May, 1958—Paramount
Produced by Hal Wallis, directed by Michael Curtiz, starring Elvis Presley, Carolyn Jones, Dolores Hart, Dean Jones, Walter Matthau.

G.I. Blues
October, 1960—Paramount
Produced by Hal Wallis, directed by Norman Taurog, starring Elvis Presley, James Douglas, Robert Ivers, Juliet Prowse.

Flaming Star
December, 1960—Twentieth Century-Fox
Produced by David Weisbart, directed by Don Siegel, starring Elvis Presley, Steve Forrest, Barbara Eden, Dolores Del Rio, John McIntyre.

Wild in the Country
June, 1961—Twentieth Century-Fox
Produced by Jerry Wald, directed by Philip Dunne, starring Elvis Presley, Hope Lange, Tuesday Weld, Millie Perkins, Rafer Johnson.

Blue Hawaii
October, 1961—Paramount
Produced by Hal Wallis, directed by Norman Taurog, starring Elvis Presley, Joan Blackman, Nancy Walters, Roland Winters, Angela Lansbury.

Follow That Dream
March, 1962—United Artists
Produced by David Weisbart, directed by Gordon Douglas, starring Elvis Presley, Arthur O'Connell, Anne Helm, Joanna Moore.

Kid Galahad
July, 1962—United Artists
Produced by David Weisbart, directed by Phil Karlson, starring Elvis Presley, Gig Young, Lola Albright, Joan Blackman, Charles Bronson.

Girls! Girls! Girls
November, 1962—Paramount
Produced by Hal Wallis, directed by Norman Taurog, starring Elvis Presley, Stella Stevens, Laurel Goodwin, Jeremy Slate.

It Happened at the World's Fair
April, 1963—MGM
Produced by Ted Richmond, directed by Norman Taurog, starring Elvis Presley, Joan O'Brien, Gary Lockwood, Vicky Tiu.

Fun in Acapulco
November, 1963—Paramount
Produced by Hal Wallis, directed by Richard Thorpe, starring Elvis Presley, Ursula Andress, Elsa Cardenas, Paul Lukas.

Kissin' Cousins
March, 1964—MGM
Produced by Sam Katzman, directed by Gene Nelson, starring Elvis Presley, Arthur O'Connell, Glenda Farrell, Jack Albertson.

Viva Las Vegas
April, 1964—MGM
Produced by Jack Cummings and George Sidney, directed by George Sidney, starring Elvis Presley, Ann-Margret, Cesare Danova, William Demarest.

Roustabout
November, 1964—Paramount
Produced by Hal Wallis, directed by John Rich, starring Elvis Presley, Barbara Stanwyck, Joan Freeman, Leif Erickson, Sue Ane Langdon.

Girl Happy
January, 1965—MGM
Produced by Joe Pasternak, directed by Boris Sagal, starring Elvis Presley, Shelly Fabares, Harold J. Stone, Gary Crosby, Mary Ann Mobley.

Tickle Me
June, 1965—Allied Artists
Produced by Ben Schwalb, directed by Norman Taurog, starring Elvis Presley, Jocelyn Lane, Julie Adams, Jack Mullaney.

Harum Scarum
December, 1965—MGM
Produced by Sam Katzman, directed by Gene Nelson, starring Elvis Presley, Mary Ann Mobley, Fran Jeffries, Michael Ansara.

Frankie and Johnny
July, 1966—United Artists
Produced by Edward Small, directed by Fred de Cordova, starring Elvis Presley, Donna Douglas, Nancy Kovack, Sue Ane Langdon.

Paradise—Hawaiian Style
June, 1966—Paramount
Produced by Hal Wallis, directed by Michael Moore, starring Elvis Presley, Suzanne Leigh, James Shigeta, Donna Butterworth.

Spinout
December, 1966—MGM
Produced by Joe Pasternak, directed by Norman Taurog, starring Elvis Presley, Shelley Fabares, Diane McBain, Deborah Walley.

Easy Come, Easy Go
March, 1967—Paramount
Produced by Hal Wallis, directed by John Rich, starring Elvis Presley, Dodie Marshall, Pat Priest, Pat Harrington

Double Trouble
May, 1967—MGM
Produced by Judd Bernard and Irwin Winkler, directed by Norman Taurog, starring Elvis Presley, Annette Day, John Williams, Yvonne Romain.

Clambake
December, 1967—United Artists
Produced by Arnold Laven, Arthur Gardner, and Jules Levy, directed by Arthur Nadel, starring Elvis Presley, Shelley Fabares, Will Hutchins, Bill Bixby.

Speedway
June, 1968—MGM
Produced by Douglas Laurence, directed by Norman Taurog, starring Elvis Presley, Nancy Sinatra, Bill Bixby, Gale Gordon, William Schallert.

Live a Little, Love a Little
October, 1968—MGM
Produced by Douglas Laurence, directed by Norman Taurog, starring Elvis Presley, Michele Carey, Don Porter, Rudy Vallee, Dick Sargent.

Charro!
September, 1969—National General
Produced and directed by Charles Marquis Warren, starring Elvis Presley, Ina Balin, Victor French.

The Trouble with Girls (and How to Get into It)
December, 1969—MGM
Produced by Lester Welch, directed by Peter Tewksbury, starring Elvis Presley, Marilyn Mason, Nicole Jaffee, Sheree North.

Change of Habit
January, 1970—NBC–Universal
Produced by Joe Connelly, directed by William Graham, starring Elvis Presley, Mary Tyler Moore, Barbara McNair, Jane Elliot, Edward Asner.

Elvis: That's the Way It Is
December, 1970—MGM
Produced by Herbert F. Soklow, directed by Denis Sanders. Documentary.

Elvis on Tour
June, 1973—MGM
Produced and directed by Pierre Adidge and Robert Abel. Documentary.

MICHAEL OCHS was born in Austin, Texas, and graduated from Ohio State University with a degree in radio and television writing. He runs the Michael Ochs Archives, a library of photographs, records, magazines, and other research materials centered around the entertainment industry. He lives in Venice, California.

STEVE POND grew up in southern California and graduated with a degree in journalism from California State University at Long Beach. He is a contributing editor of *Rolling Stone* and *Premier*, and he has a weekly column in the *Washington Post*. He lives in Los Angeles.